MAD LIBS®

GONE FISHING MAD LIBS

by Stacy Wasserman

MAD LIBS
An imprint of Penguin Random House LLC, New York

First published in the United States of America by Mad Libs,
an imprint of Penguin Random House LLC, New York, 2024

Mad Libs format and text copyright © 2024 by Penguin Random House LLC

Concept created by Roger Price & Leonard Stern

Cover illustration by Scott Brooks

Penguin supports copyright. Copyright fuels creativity, encourages diverse voices,
promotes free speech, and creates a vibrant culture. Thank you for buying an authorized
edition of this book and for complying with copyright laws by not reproducing, scanning,
or distributing any part of it in any form without permission. You are supporting writers
and allowing Penguin to continue to publish books for every reader.

MAD LIBS and logo are registered trademarks of Penguin Random House LLC.

Visit us online at penguinrandomhouse.com.

Printed in the United States of America

ISBN 9780593658642
1 3 5 7 9 10 8 6 4 2
COMR

MAD LIBS
INSTRUCTIONS

MAD LIBS® is a game for people who don't like games! It can be played by one, two, three, four, or forty.

• RIDICULOUSLY SIMPLE DIRECTIONS

In this tablet you will find stories containing blank spaces where words are left out. One player, the READER, selects one of these stories. The READER does not tell anyone what the story is about. Instead, he/she asks the other players, the WRITERS, to give him/her words. These words are used to fill in the blank spaces in the story.

• TO PLAY

The READER asks each WRITER in turn to call out a word—an adjective or a noun or whatever the space calls for—and uses them to fill in the blank spaces in the story. The result is a MAD LIBS® game.

When the READER then reads the completed MAD LIBS® game to the other players, they will discover that they have written a story that is fantastic, screamingly funny, shocking, silly, crazy, or just plain dumb—depending upon which words each WRITER called out.

• EXAMPLE (*Before* and *After*)

"_____!" he said _____
    EXCLAMATION   ADVERB

as he jumped into his convertible _____ and
                                      NOUN

drove off with his _____ wife.
                     ADJECTIVE

"____**OUCH**____!" he said ____**HAPPILY**____
   EXCLAMATION   ADVERB

as he jumped into his convertible ____**CAT**____ and
                                   NOUN

drove off with his ____**BRAVE**____ wife.
                 ADJECTIVE

MAD LIBS
QUICK REVIEW

In case you have forgotten what adjectives, adverbs, nouns, and verbs are, here is a quick review:

An ADJECTIVE describes something or somebody. *Lumpy*, *soft*, *ugly*, *messy*, and *short* are adjectives.

An ADVERB tells how something is done. It modifies a verb and usually ends in "ly." *Modestly*, *stupidly*, *greedily*, and *carefully* are adverbs.

A NOUN is the name of a person, place, or thing. *Sidewalk*, *umbrella*, *bridle*, *bathtub*, and *nose* are nouns.

A VERB is an action word. *Run*, *pitch*, *jump*, and *swim* are verbs. Put the verbs in past tense if the directions say PAST TENSE. *Ran*, *pitched*, *jumped*, and *swam* are verbs in the past tense.

When we ask for A PLACE, we mean any sort of place: a country or city (*Spain*, *Cleveland*) or a room (*bathroom*, *kitchen*).

An EXCLAMATION or SILLY WORD is any sort of funny sound, gasp, grunt, or outcry, like *Wow!*, *Ouch!*, *Whomp!*, *Ick!*, and *Gadzooks!*

When we ask for specific words, like a NUMBER, a COLOR, an ANIMAL, or a PART OF THE BODY, we mean a word that is one of those things, like *seven*, *blue*, *horse*, or *head*.

When we ask for a PLURAL, it means more than one. For example, *cat* pluralized is *cats*.

MAD LIBS® is fun to play with friends, but you can also play it by yourself! To begin with, DO NOT look at the story on the page below. Fill in the blanks on this page with the words called for. Then, using the words you have selected, fill in the blank spaces in the story.

Now you've created your own hilarious MAD LIBS® game!

LET'S GO FISHING

PERSON YOU KNOW _____

VERB _____

NUMBER _____

TYPE OF LIQUID _____

NOUN _____

VERB _____

ADJECTIVE _____

VERB ENDING IN "ING" _____

ANIMAL _____

PLURAL NOUN _____

VERB _____

VERB ENDING IN "ING" _____

NOUN _____

PART OF THE BODY _____

NOUN _____

ADJECTIVE _____

NOUN _____

A PLACE _____

MAD LIBS

LET'S GO FISHING

_____ and I are going fishing today. I absolutely love
PERSON YOU KNOW

to _____. It is my all-time number _____ favorite
     VERB   NUMBER

activity. There's nothing like being out on the _____
                                                                      TYPE OF LIQUID

under the summer _____. Even if we don't _____
                           NOUN   VERB

anything, I just love being out in the _____ outdoors!
                                             ADJECTIVE

Of course, it *is* better when the fish are _____.
                                                      VERB ENDING IN "ING"

Catching the first _____ of the day is always a thrill,
                         ANIMAL

but sometimes having to wait for a bite can add to the excitement.

While you're waiting, don't let your _____ wander
                                         PLURAL NOUN

or _____ your guard. And never forget that you're
         VERB

_____. Otherwise, you might find yourself saying,
VERB ENDING IN "ING"

"Was that a tug on the end of my _____?!?" When you
                                     NOUN

get a bite, your _____ will start beating like a/an
                   PART OF THE BODY

_____. It's so exciting when a/an _____ fish is
 NOUN   ADJECTIVE

at the end of your line! And it only gets better when you reel in your

catch with your trusty fishing _____. I tell you, there's
                                      NOUN

no feeling like it in the whole wide _____.
                                         A PLACE

From GONE FISHING MAD LIBS® • Copyright © 2024 by Penguin Random House LLC

MAD LIBS® is fun to play with friends, but you can also play it by yourself! To begin with, DO NOT look at the story on the page below. Fill in the blanks on this page with the words called for. Then, using the words you have selected, fill in the blank spaces in the story.

Now you've created your own hilarious MAD LIBS® game!

THE CATCH OF THE DAY

VERB (PAST TENSE) _____

CITY _____

SOMETHING ALIVE _____

NUMBER _____

ADJECTIVE _____

NOUN _____

ARTICLE OF CLOTHING _____

VERB _____

NUMBER _____

PLURAL NOUN _____

PART OF THE BODY _____

ANIMAL _____

VERB _____

VEHICLE _____

VERB ENDING IN "ING" _____

VERB _____

SOMETHING ALIVE _____

MAD LIBS

THE CATCH OF THE DAY

Today, I _____ the biggest fish anyone in _____
      VERB (PAST TENSE)   CITY

has ever seen! It's too bad that I was the only _____ on
                                                             SOMETHING ALIVE

my boat to see it, because it must have been _____ feet long!
                                                          NUMBER

I would have taken a selfie with the _____ fish, but I forgot
                                            ADJECTIVE

my _____ at home. It seems I never have my cell phone in
      NOUN

my _____ pocket when I really need to _____
     ARTICLE OF CLOTHING   VERB

it. Anyway, this fish was sooooo big, it must have weighed as much

as _____ _____. I'm just lucky that the muscles
    NUMBER   PLURAL NOUN

in my _____ are huge, too! Because if I wasn't as strong
        PART OF THE BODY

as a/an _____, there's no way I would have been able
           ANIMAL

to _____ that fish into my fishing _____.
     VERB   VEHICLE

I really wish I could show you the actual fish, but I gave it to a group

of schoolchildren who were _____ in the harbor on
                             VERB ENDING IN "ING"

a class field trip! What can I _____? That's just the kind
                                VERB

of _____ I am!
   SOMETHING ALIVE

From GONE FISHING MAD LIBS® • Copyright © 2024 by Penguin Random House LLC

MAD LIBS® is fun to play with friends, but you can also play it by yourself! To begin with, DO NOT look at the story on the page below. Fill in the blanks on this page with the words called for. Then, using the words you have selected, fill in the blank spaces in the story.

Now you've created your own hilarious MAD LIBS® game!

FISH TALES

EXCLAMATION _____

ANIMAL (PLURAL) _____

NUMBER _____

VERB _____

TYPE OF LIQUID _____

VERB _____

NUMBER _____

TYPE OF FOOD (PLURAL) _____

VERB _____

ADJECTIVE _____

ANIMAL _____

A PLACE _____

VERB (PAST TENSE) _____

SILLY WORD _____

PART OF THE BODY _____

OCCUPATION _____

VERB _____

MAD LIBS

FISH TALES

Friend #1: _____! Were the _____
        EXCLAMATION   ANIMAL (PLURAL)

biting today! I caught _____ before lunch.
                        NUMBER

Friend #2: _____ me about it. I caught so many fish,
              VERB

I could barely keep my line in the _____.
                                    TYPE OF LIQUID

Friend #1: I know! After lunch, all I did was _____
                                                   VERB

and _____ fish jumped right into the boat. It was totally
      NUMBER

_____!
TYPE OF FOOD (PLURAL)

Friend #2: I can _____ that. There I was reeling in a/an
                     VERB

_____ one—a real fighter—when another _____
ADJECTIVE   ANIMAL

jumped right out of (the) _____ and into my arms. It really
                           A PLACE

_____ me by surprise.
VERB (PAST TENSE)

Friend #1: Oh, _____! Now you're just pulling my
                   SILLY WORD

_____.
PART OF THE BODY

Friend #2: _____'s honor. Really, I swear. May I never
              OCCUPATION

_____ another fish if I'm lying.
VERB

From GONE FISHING MAD LIBS® • Copyright © 2024 by Penguin Random House LLC

MAD LIBS® is fun to play with friends, but you can also play it by yourself! To begin with, DO NOT look at the story on the page below. Fill in the blanks on this page with the words called for. Then, using the words you have selected, fill in the blank spaces in the story.

Now you've created your own hilarious MAD LIBS® game!

SOMETHING'S FISHY!

PERSON YOU KNOW _____

OCCUPATION _____

ADJECTIVE _____

NOUN _____

PART OF THE BODY _____

PLURAL NOUN _____

ADJECTIVE _____

NUMBER _____

PLURAL NOUN _____

ADJECTIVE _____

VERB ENDING IN "ING" _____

ANIMAL _____

TYPE OF LIQUID (PLURAL) _____

COUNTRY _____

NOUN _____

VERB ENDING IN "ING" _____

ADJECTIVE _____

MAD LIBS

SOMETHING'S FISHY!

Hey there! _____ here to tell you a little bit about what I
            PERSON YOU KNOW

do. I'm an Alaskan _____, and my job is considered one of
                  OCCUPATION

the most _____ jobs in the world. We risk our _____
          ADJECTIVE   NOUN

and _____ hauling up nets and cages that weigh as
       PART OF THE BODY

much as hundreds and hundreds of _____. Believe
                                            PLURAL NOUN

me, it's _____ work. Add on _____-foot waves,
         ADJECTIVE   NUMBER

icy _____, and _____ temperatures and
    PLURAL NOUN   ADJECTIVE

this job can become even more dangerous. The most unsafe type of

Alaskan _____ is _____ fishing. This job
        VERB ENDING IN "ING"   ANIMAL

takes place far out in the _____ found between
                              TYPE OF LIQUID (PLURAL)

Alaska and _____. As if that's not dangerous enough,
                COUNTRY

these fishermen work in the dark. The _____ only rises
                                              NOUN

in the sky for a few hours each day at that time of year. I love my job

and I love _____, but not even I'm _____
         VERB ENDING IN "ING"   ADJECTIVE

enough to do that.

From GONE FISHING MAD LIBS® • Copyright © 2024 by Penguin Random House LLC

MAD LIBS® is fun to play with friends, but you can also play it by yourself! To begin with, DO NOT look at the story on the page below. Fill in the blanks on this page with the words called for. Then, using the words you have selected, fill in the blank spaces in the story.

Now you've created your own hilarious MAD LIBS® game!

TACKLE BOX TREASURES

LETTER OF THE ALPHABET _____

ADJECTIVE _____

TYPE OF CONTAINER _____

ADJECTIVE _____

VERB _____

NOUN _____

SAME NOUN _____

COLOR _____

NUMBER _____

PLURAL NOUN _____

VERB ENDING IN "ING" _____

ADJECTIVE _____

ANIMAL (PLURAL) _____

NOUN _____

TYPE OF FOOD _____

VERB _____

MAD LIBS®

TACKLE BOX TREASURES

O-M- _____ ! I am so _____ about my
    LETTER OF THE ALPHABET   ADJECTIVE

brand-new tackle _____. When I first started fishing,
                    TYPE OF CONTAINER

I used to just use a/an _____ bag to carry around all of my
                      ADJECTIVE

supplies, but it was such a mess and I could never _____
                                                VERB

the fishing gear I needed. Now there's a proper _____
                                                  NOUN

for everything and everything has its _____. It's my
                                        SAME NOUN

favorite shade of _____ and has an upper compartment
                         COLOR

and _____ drawers. In the drawers, I've organized all of my fishing
     NUMBER

_____ by type. In the top, I keep extra fishing lures,
  PLURAL NOUN

extra _____ line, and any _____ tools
      VERB ENDING IN "ING"   ADJECTIVE

I might need. A ruler is particularly important for measuring the

_____ we catch. And the best part of my new tackle
 ANIMAL (PLURAL)

box is the "secret" _____ in the lid. That's where I keep all
                          NOUN

the good snacks like _____ and chips. You can have
                        TYPE OF FOOD

some. But don't _____ anybody!
                VERB

From GONE FISHING MAD LIBS® • Copyright © 2024 by Penguin Random House LLC

MAD LIBS® is fun to play with friends, but you can also play it by yourself! To begin with, DO NOT look at the story on the page below. Fill in the blanks on this page with the words called for. Then, using the words you have selected, fill in the blank spaces in the story.

Now you've created your own hilarious MAD LIBS® game!

FISHING FOR HISTORY

ADJECTIVE _____

NUMBER _____

OCCUPATION (PLURAL) _____

SILLY WORD _____

A PLACE _____

ANIMAL (PLURAL) _____

VERB (PAST TENSE) _____

TYPE OF FOOD _____

PART OF THE BODY (PLURAL) _____

ADJECTIVE _____

PLURAL NOUN _____

VERB ENDING IN "ING" _____

PLURAL NOUN _____

PLURAL NOUN _____

ADJECTIVE _____

VERB _____

PLURAL NOUN _____

VERB ENDING IN "S" _____

MAD LIBS
FISHING FOR HISTORY

Fishing is a/an _____ practice known to have started over
                    ADJECTIVE
_____ years ago among early humans, called *Homo sapiens*.
   NUMBER
However, some _____ argue that fishing goes back
                 OCCUPATION (PLURAL)
even farther than that to our ancestors *Homo* _____.
                                                  SILLY WORD
As with many mammals in the animal _____, early
                                         A PLACE
_____ fished as a means of survival. Our ancestors
 ANIMAL (PLURAL)
_____ to eat and traded their _____ for other
VERB (PAST TENSE)   TYPE OF FOOD
goods. At first, they only used their _____ to catch
                                         PART OF THE BODY (PLURAL)
fish. Then they developed _____ _____ to help
                            ADJECTIVE   PLURAL NOUN
them. Amazingly, some of the oldest tools for _____
                                                 VERB ENDING IN "ING"
are still used today, such as nets, spears with barbed _____
                                                          PLURAL NOUN
called harpoons, and even fishing _____. I guess if it
                                      PLURAL NOUN
ain't _____, why fix it? It just goes to _____ you that
       ADJECTIVE   VERB
despite all of our technological _____, when it comes to
                                    PLURAL NOUN
fishing, people stick with what _____.
                                  VERB ENDING IN "S"

From GONE FISHING MAD LIBS® • Copyright © 2024 by Penguin Random House LLC

MAD LIBS® is fun to play with friends, but you can also play it by yourself! To begin with, DO NOT look at the story on the page below. Fill in the blanks on this page with the words called for. Then, using the words you have selected, fill in the blank spaces in the story.

Now you've created your own hilarious MAD LIBS® game!

THE ONE THAT GOT AWAY, PART 1

PART OF THE BODY _____

ADJECTIVE _____

COLOR _____

ANIMAL _____

NUMBER _____

OCCUPATION (PLURAL) _____

NOUN _____

VERB ENDING IN "ING" _____

ADJECTIVE _____

VERB (PAST TENSE) _____

VERB _____

NUMBER _____

EXCLAMATION _____

ADJECTIVE _____

ADJECTIVE _____

VERB (PAST TENSE) _____

MAD LIBS
THE ONE THAT GOT AWAY, PART 1

With a trembling _____ I begin my tale
         PART OF THE BODY
about a fish more wicked than
a/an _____ _____ whale.
         ADJECTIVE   COLOR
No normal _____, this creature is beyond reason.
              ANIMAL
He haunts the _____ seas during every season!
                  NUMBER
An enemy of _____ since the _____ of time;
             OCCUPATION (PLURAL)   NOUN
he escapes _____ nets because he's covered in slime.
           VERB ENDING IN "ING"
And I, _____ I, am no exception to that rule,
        ADJECTIVE
for this fish has _____ me the classic fool.
                   VERB (PAST TENSE)
Will you _____ my tale about the fish named Flounder?
           VERB
I swear he must be bigger than a/an _____-pounder!
                                      NUMBER
_____, it is _____ how much there is to say
 EXCLAMATION   ADJECTIVE
about the _____ fish that _____ away.
            ADJECTIVE   VERB (PAST TENSE)

From GONE FISHING MAD LIBS® • Copyright © 2024 by Penguin Random House LLC

MAD LIBS® is fun to play with friends, but you can also play it by yourself! To begin with, DO NOT look at the story on the page below. Fill in the blanks on this page with the words called for. Then, using the words you have selected, fill in the blank spaces in the story.

Now you've created your own hilarious MAD LIBS® game!

WE'RE GONNA NEED A BIGGER BOAT

ADJECTIVE _____

PART OF THE BODY _____

NOUN _____

NUMBER _____

VERB _____

ADJECTIVE _____

NOUN _____

TYPE OF CONTAINER _____

COLOR _____

VEHICLE _____

PART OF THE BODY _____

EXCLAMATION _____

ADJECTIVE _____

OCCUPATION _____

NOUN _____

VERB ENDING IN "ING" _____

ADJECTIVE _____

TYPE OF FOOD _____

MAD LIBS®
WE'RE GONNA NEED A BIGGER BOAT

The _____ shark circled our dive boat with its triangle-
         ADJECTIVE
shaped _____ cutting through the waves. This was
       PART OF THE BODY
the _____ I had been waiting for ever since I became
        NOUN
an underwater photographer _____ years ago! What can
                                 NUMBER
I _____? Some people like to catch fish, but the only
     VERB
thing I like to catch is . . . the _____ photograph! I pulled
                                       ADJECTIVE
my scuba _____ over my face and plunged into the shark
          NOUN
_____. From underwater, the great _____
TYPE OF CONTAINER   COLOR
shark looked even bigger. It was the size of a school _____!
                                                          VEHICLE
I watched as it stared at me with its _____. I
                                       PART OF THE BODY
could almost hear the shark thinking, "_____, that
                                         EXCLAMATION
_____ _____ looks delicious!" As the shark swam
   ADJECTIVE   OCCUPATION
close to the cage, I used my _____ to take as many pictures
                                NOUN
as I could, even though my hands were _____. And
                                       VERB ENDING IN "ING"
when I looked down at my camera, I could see I got the perfect shot!
It looked like the shark was smiling at me with its rows and rows of
_____ teeth! "Say _____!"
   ADJECTIVE   TYPE OF FOOD

From GONE FISHING MAD LIBS® • Copyright © 2024 by Penguin Random House LLC

MAD LIBS® is fun to play with friends, but you can also play it by yourself! To begin with, DO NOT look at the story on the page below. Fill in the blanks on this page with the words called for. Then, using the words you have selected, fill in the blank spaces in the story.

Now you've created your own hilarious MAD LIBS® game!

FAMOUS FISHING STORIES

NOUN _____

OCCUPATION (PLURAL) _____

ADJECTIVE _____

VERB (PAST TENSE) _____

FIRST NAME _____

PERSON YOU KNOW _____

ADJECTIVE _____

COLOR _____

ANIMAL _____

PART OF THE BODY _____

ADJECTIVE _____

CELEBRITY _____

OCCUPATION _____

NOUN _____

A PLACE _____

ADJECTIVE _____

A PLACE _____

VERB ENDING IN "ING" _____

MAD LIBS
FAMOUS FISHING STORIES

Ever since the very first stories were printed on the pages of a/an

_____ , _____ have written _____
   NOUN   OCCUPATION (PLURAL)   ADJECTIVE

stories about fishing. Here are some of the greatest fish tales ever

_____:
VERB (PAST TENSE)

- **Moby** _____ by _____ is a book about
             FIRST NAME   PERSON YOU KNOW

  a/an _____ sea captain seeking revenge on a/an
         ADJECTIVE

  _____ _____ who destroyed his ship and
    COLOR   ANIMAL

  bit off his _____.
            PART OF THE BODY

- **The** _____ **Man and the Sea** by _____ is
       ADJECTIVE   CELEBRITY

  the story of an unlucky _____ and his epic struggle to
                 OCCUPATION

  catch a huge marlin with a nose shaped like a/an _____.
                                                                              NOUN

- **A/An** _____ **Runs Through It** by Norman
         A PLACE

  Mac-_____ is a story about brothers growing up in a
      ADJECTIVE

  small _____ in Montana and the pastime that brings
       A PLACE

  them together: _____.
                     VERB ENDING IN "ING"

From GONE FISHING MAD LIBS® • Copyright © 2024 by Penguin Random House LLC

MAD LIBS® is fun to play with friends, but you can also play it by yourself! To begin with, DO NOT look at the story on the page below. Fill in the blanks on this page with the words called for. Then, using the words you have selected, fill in the blank spaces in the story.

Now you've created your own hilarious MAD LIBS® game!

FISHING QUIZ

OCCUPATION _____

VERB _____

VERB ENDING IN "ING" _____

ADJECTIVE _____

NUMBER _____

TYPE OF CONTAINER _____

ANIMAL (PLURAL) _____

EXCLAMATION _____

PLURAL NOUN _____

SILLY WORD _____

ARTICLE OF CLOTHING (PLURAL) _____

ADJECTIVE _____

VERB ENDING IN "ING" _____

NOUN _____

A PLACE _____

MAD LIBS
FISHING QUIZ

Are you a true _____? _____ this quiz to find
           OCCUPATION   VERB
out how much you love fishing.

1. The best time to go fishing is: (a) in the morning when the fish
   are _____, (b) at night when the waves are
         VERB ENDING IN "ING"
   _____, (c) all the time
       ADJECTIVE

2. How many fish do you have to catch in order to have a great day?
   (a) between one and _____, (b) just enough to fill
                            NUMBER
   a/an _____, (c) it really doesn't matter how many
         TYPE OF CONTAINER
   _____ you catch!
      ANIMAL (PLURAL)

3. When you catch a fish, what do you say? (a) _____!
                                                   EXCLAMATION
   (b) Oh my _____! (c) _____!
                PLURAL NOUN   SILLY WORD

Answer Key: Mostly *a*'s: You like fishing about as much as you like
folding _____. Mostly *b*'s: Sure, fishing is
         ARTICLE OF CLOTHING (PLURAL)
_____, but the bumper sticker on your car reads "I'd rather
   ADJECTIVE
be _____." Mostly *c*'s: You love fishing more than your
      VERB ENDING IN "ING"
favorite _____. You'd go fishing in (the) _____
             NOUN   A PLACE
if you could!

From GONE FISHING MAD LIBS® • Copyright © 2024 by Penguin Random House LLC

MAD LIBS® is fun to play with friends, but you can also play it by yourself! To begin with, DO NOT look at the story on the page below. Fill in the blanks on this page with the words called for. Then, using the words you have selected, fill in the blank spaces in the story.

Now you've created your own hilarious MAD LIBS® game!

WHOSE LINE IS IT?

EXCLAMATION _____

A PLACE _____

NOUN _____

VERB (PAST TENSE) _____

PART OF THE BODY _____

TYPE OF CONTAINER _____

TYPE OF FOOD _____

ANIMAL _____

VERB _____

ADJECTIVE _____

SOMETHING ALIVE (PLURAL) _____

ARTICLE OF CLOTHING _____

VERB (PAST TENSE) _____

TYPE OF LIQUID _____

ANIMAL _____

VERB ENDING IN "ING" _____

MAD LIBS®
WHOSE LINE IS IT?

_____, I am not meant for fishing! From the moment we
EXCLAMATION

got to (the) _____, it was just one _____
             A PLACE   NOUN

after another. First, I _____ on someone else's fishing
                        VERB (PAST TENSE)

rod, landed on my _____, and spilled the contents
                   PART OF THE BODY

of my lunch _____ all over the pier. The seagulls ate
             TYPE OF CONTAINER

my _____ sandwich! Then, it took me forever to cast
    TYPE OF FOOD

my hook with the rubber _____ on it into the water.
                          ANIMAL

Turns out, it's really important to _____ behind you
                                     VERB

before you cast your line! I almost hooked several _____
                                                    ADJECTIVE

_____ walking by! But I did manage to hook my
SOMETHING ALIVE (PLURAL)

own baseball _____ and it _____ over
              ARTICLE OF CLOTHING   VERB (PAST TENSE)

the railing. Eventually I got my line in the _____. Not
                                               TYPE OF LIQUID

that it mattered since I didn't catch a single _____—all day
                                                 ANIMAL

long! I'm never going _____ again!
                       VERB ENDING IN "ING"

From GONE FISHING MAD LIBS® • Copyright © 2024 by Penguin Random House LLC

MAD LIBS® is fun to play with friends, but you can also play it by yourself! To begin with, DO NOT look at the story on the page below. Fill in the blanks on this page with the words called for. Then, using the words you have selected, fill in the blank spaces in the story.

Now you've created your own hilarious MAD LIBS® game!

CAMP FIELD TRIP

ADJECTIVE _____

ANIMAL (PLURAL) _____

OCCUPATION _____

VERB ENDING IN "ING" _____

TYPE OF BUILDING _____

NOUN _____

VERB _____

PART OF THE BODY (PLURAL) _____

SILLY WORD _____

VERB ENDING IN "ING" _____

PLURAL NOUN _____

TYPE OF LIQUID _____

TYPE OF FOOD _____

VERB _____

VEHICLE (PLURAL) _____

VERB _____

MAD LIBS

CAMP FIELD TRIP

It's six o'clock in the morning. Everyone at the _____
                                                    ADJECTIVE
_____ Sleepaway Camp is going on a surprise fishing
ANIMAL (PLURAL)
trip today, and I'm the _____ in charge of getting
                              OCCUPATION
the campers to the boat on time. I've already placed our buckets
and _____ rods by the front door of our log
       VERB ENDING IN "ING"
_____, so we don't forget anything. Then, I ring
TYPE OF BUILDING
the camp _____ and make an announcement to the
              NOUN
students! "Good morning, campers! _____ and shine,
                                            VERB
sleepy-_____." But no one responds. So, I
          PART OF THE BODY (PLURAL)
try again. "Wakey-_____, everybody! We're going
                          SILLY WORD
_____ today!" Suddenly, the excited campers jump
VERB ENDING IN "ING"
out of their bunk _____ and grab their _____
                        PLURAL NOUN   TYPE OF LIQUID
bottles and some _____ bars for lunch. I've never seen
                        TYPE OF FOOD
them _____ this fast before. They must like fishing trips
          VERB
as much as they like going to ride the roller _____
                                                          VEHICLE (PLURAL)
at the amusement park! And the best part is, the fishing trip doesn't
make me _____ upside down on the loop the loops!
                VERB

From GONE FISHING MAD LIBS® • Copyright © 2024 by Penguin Random House LLC

MAD LIBS® is fun to play with friends, but you can also play it by yourself! To begin with, DO NOT look at the story on the page below. Fill in the blanks on this page with the words called for. Then, using the words you have selected, fill in the blank spaces in the story.

Now you've created your own hilarious MAD LIBS® game!

THE ONE THAT GOT AWAY, PART 2

NUMBER _____

ANIMAL _____

ADJECTIVE _____

OCCUPATION (PLURAL) _____

PLURAL NOUN _____

VERB (PAST TENSE) _____

ADJECTIVE _____

VERB ENDING IN "S" _____

PART OF THE BODY (PLURAL) _____

ADJECTIVE _____

TYPE OF FOOD _____

VERB _____

VERB ENDING IN "ING" _____

VEHICLE _____

FIRST NAME _____

MAD LIBS
THE ONE THAT GOT AWAY, PART 2

This is part _____ of the poem about Flounder,
NUMBER

the _____ that got away.
ANIMAL

You are a/an _____ and slippery fish,
ADJECTIVE

that's what all the _____ say.
OCCUPATION (PLURAL)

You've wiggled out of nylon _____
PLURAL NOUN

and _____ around all our hooks.
VERB (PAST TENSE)

You're a sneaky, _____ fish
ADJECTIVE

that _____ in the record books!
VERB ENDING IN "S"

No one knows what makes you so uncatchable.

Could it be your _____ or _____ eyes?
PART OF THE BODY (PLURAL)   ADJECTIVE

Or maybe it's your tiny _____ -size brain
TYPE OF FOOD

that makes you so very wise.

And if I ever _____ you, Flounder,
VERB

while _____ on a/an _____
VERB ENDING IN "ING"   VEHICLE

some summer's day,

I promise to set you free, _____ ,
FIRST NAME

because you're the one that got away.

From GONE FISHING MAD LIBS® • Copyright © 2024 by Penguin Random House LLC

MAD LIBS® is fun to play with friends, but you can also play it by yourself! To begin with, DO NOT look at the story on the page below. Fill in the blanks on this page with the words called for. Then, using the words you have selected, fill in the blank spaces in the story.

Now you've created your own hilarious MAD LIBS® game!

FUN FACTS ABOUT FISH

TYPE OF LIQUID _____

ADJECTIVE _____

SOMETHING ALIVE (PLURAL) _____

VERB (PAST TENSE) _____

ADJECTIVE _____

ANIMAL (PLURAL) _____

VERB _____

PART OF THE BODY _____

ANIMAL _____

NUMBER _____

PLURAL NOUN _____

ANIMAL (PLURAL) _____

PLURAL NOUN _____

NOUN _____

PART OF THE BODY _____

VERB ENDING IN "ING" _____

MAD LIBS

FUN FACTS ABOUT FISH

Did you know a fish can drown in _____ without
                                     TYPE OF LIQUID

enough oxygen? Check out these other _____ fish facts
                                          ADJECTIVE

you might not know:

1. Just like _____, some fish can get sun-
              SOMETHING ALIVE (PLURAL)

   _____ if exposed to _____ periods of
   VERB (PAST TENSE)   ADJECTIVE

   direct sunlight. Talk about fried _____!
                                          ANIMAL (PLURAL)

2. Fish don't just _____ food with their _____,
                        VERB   PART OF THE BODY

   they taste with their body, too. _____-fish have the
                                              ANIMAL

   best sense of taste of any animal and _____ times more taste
                                              NUMBER

   _____ than humans.
     PLURAL NOUN

3. Despite their names, both starfish and jellyfish are not actually

   _____. Their more accurate names are sea
       ANIMAL (PLURAL)

   _____ and _____ jellies.
     PLURAL NOUN   NOUN

4. Some fish don't have _____-lids—so they can't
                              PART OF THE BODY

   blink! I know who'd win that _____ contest.
                                     VERB ENDING IN "ING"

From GONE FISHING MAD LIBS® • Copyright © 2024 by Penguin Random House LLC

MAD LIBS® is fun to play with friends, but you can also play it by yourself! To begin with, DO NOT look at the story on the page below. Fill in the blanks on this page with the words called for. Then, using the words you have selected, fill in the blank spaces in the story.

Now you've created your own hilarious MAD LIBS® game!

DOG DAYS OF SUMMER

CELEBRITY _____

PLURAL NOUN _____

ANIMAL (PLURAL) _____

SAME PLURAL NOUN _____

VERB _____

ANIMAL (PLURAL) _____

VERB ENDING IN "ING" _____

SAME CELEBRITY _____

PART OF THE BODY _____

TYPE OF FOOD _____

VERB (PAST TENSE) _____

COLOR _____

PLURAL NOUN _____

VERB ENDING IN "ING" _____

EXCLAMATION _____

OCCUPATION _____

NOUN _____

PLURAL NOUN _____

MAD LIBS

DOG DAYS OF SUMMER

I love spending the day at the beach fishing with my dog. His name is _____ , but we call him _____ for
      CELEBRITY   PLURAL NOUN

short. In the mornings, I like to sit and read while we wait for the

_____ to bite. During this time, _____
  ANIMAL (PLURAL)   SAME PLURAL NOUN

loves to _____ in the water, roll around in the sand, and
            VERB

chase the sea-_____. Talk about _____
                   ANIMAL (PLURAL)   VERB ENDING IN "ING"

your best life. And by the time _____ is ready for a
                                        SAME CELEBRITY

break, my _____ has started to rumble. For lunch, we
          PART OF THE BODY

share cold _____ sandwiches or _____
          TYPE OF FOOD   VERB (PAST TENSE)

cheese. And when we actually catch a fish, we look like we've won

a/an _____ medal at the Olympics. He runs in
          COLOR

_____ around me barking and _____
  PLURAL NOUN   VERB ENDING IN "ING"

his tail while I reel in the catch and yell, " _____! I'm
                                                EXCLAMATION

the best _____ to ever hold a/an _____ !"
          OCCUPATION   NOUN

I hope these summer _____ last forever!
                            PLURAL NOUN

From GONE FISHING MAD LIBS® • Copyright © 2024 by Penguin Random House LLC

MAD LIBS® is fun to play with friends, but you can also play it by yourself! To begin with, DO NOT look at the story on the page below. Fill in the blanks on this page with the words called for. Then, using the words you have selected, fill in the blank spaces in the story.

Now you've created your own hilarious MAD LIBS® game!

LETTER FROM A FISH

PERSON YOU KNOW _____

VERB ENDING IN "ING" _____

ARTICLE OF CLOTHING _____

TYPE OF BUILDING _____

PLURAL NOUN _____

ANIMAL (PLURAL) _____

VERB _____

NOUN _____

VERB _____

NOUN _____

SILLY WORD _____

ADJECTIVE _____

VERB ENDING IN "ING" _____

ADJECTIVE _____

VERB _____

SOMETHING ALIVE _____

FIRST NAME _____

MAD LIBS®

LETTER FROM A FISH

Dear _____,
    PERSON YOU KNOW

I've seen you out on the _____ pier, wearing that
                                   VERB ENDING IN "ING"

special fishing _____ you got on sale at the sports
                    ARTICLE OF CLOTHING

_____. You know, the one with all the pockets full of
TYPE OF BUILDING

tempting hooks that are disguised to look like pretty _____
                                                                    PLURAL NOUN

and tasty _____. That's right! I'm on to you! I know
          ANIMAL (PLURAL)

that you want to _____ me for dinner! So, I'm writing
                 VERB

to say I'm not falling for that old _____! If you want
                                    NOUN

to catch me, you're going to have to _____ because I'm
                                      VERB

never gonna end up on your dinner _____ drenched in
                                    NOUN

_____ sauce. I like my _____ filets right where
SILLY WORD   ADJECTIVE

they are, thank you very much! BTW, have you ever considered

_____ a vegetarian? I only eat algae, and it's not as
VERB ENDING IN "ING"

_____ as you may think! You should try it sometime!
ADJECTIVE

_____ you at the pier!
VERB

Your scaley _____,
              SOMETHING ALIVE

_____ the fish
FIRST NAME

From GONE FISHING MAD LIBS® • Copyright © 2024 by Penguin Random House LLC

MAD LIBS® is fun to play with friends, but you can also play it by yourself! To begin with, DO NOT look at the story on the page below. Fill in the blanks on this page with the words called for. Then, using the words you have selected, fill in the blank spaces in the story.

Now you've created your own hilarious MAD LIBS® game!

HOOK, LINE, AND STINKER

ADJECTIVE _____

NOUN _____

COUNTRY _____

NUMBER _____

ARTICLE OF CLOTHING (PLURAL) _____

SOMETHING ALIVE (PLURAL) _____

OCCUPATION (PLURAL) _____

TYPE OF FOOD (PLURAL) _____

TYPE OF CONTAINER _____

VEHICLE (PLURAL) _____

ADJECTIVE _____

VERB _____

TYPE OF BUILDING _____

TYPE OF FOOD (PLURAL) _____

ADJECTIVE _____

TYPE OF LIQUID _____

ADJECTIVE _____

MAD LIBS
HOOK, LINE, AND STINKER

Lots of fish are smelly! But some fish are more _____
                                                    ADJECTIVE
than others! Many countries, like _____-land, Japan,
                                       NOUN
and _____, ferment fish for _____ months
        COUNTRY   NUMBER
or more, which can give the fish an odor that smells a lot like dirty

_____. But most _____ and
ARTICLE OF CLOTHING (PLURAL)   SOMETHING ALIVE (PLURAL)

_____ agree that the smelliest fish dish in the world
OCCUPATION (PLURAL)
is from Sweden. It's called Surströmming, and it smells like rotten

_____ when you open the _____! It's
TYPE OF FOOD (PLURAL)   TYPE OF CONTAINER
so smelly that many airlines won't allow passengers to carry the fish

on their _____. Because of the _____ smell
         VEHICLE (PLURAL)   ADJECTIVE
of the fish, most people only _____ the fish when they
                                   VERB
are outside their _____. It's often served with boiled
                  TYPE OF BUILDING

_____, _____ onions, and a glass of cold
TYPE OF FOOD (PLURAL) ADJECTIVE

_____, which is supposed to balance the _____
TYPE OF LIQUID   ADJECTIVE
smell of the fish! Pee-yew!

From GONE FISHING MAD LIBS® • Copyright © 2024 by Penguin Random House LLC

MAD LIBS® is fun to play with friends, but you can also play it by yourself! To begin with, DO NOT look at the story on the page below. Fill in the blanks on this page with the words called for. Then, using the words you have selected, fill in the blank spaces in the story.

Now you've created your own hilarious MAD LIBS® game!

THE BIGGEST CATCH EVER

VERB (PAST TENSE) _____

ANIMAL _____

VERB _____

ADJECTIVE _____

A PLACE _____

PLURAL NOUN _____

ADVERB _____

ADJECTIVE _____

VERB ENDING IN "ING" _____

VERB _____

ADJECTIVE _____

NOUN _____

PERSON YOU KNOW _____

ADJECTIVE _____

ANIMAL _____

EXCLAMATION _____

NOUN _____

SILLY WORD _____

MAD LIBS

THE BIGGEST CATCH EVER

Reporter: Mr. Scaley, you have just _____ the biggest
                                         VERB (PAST TENSE)

_____ in the world. How do you _____ ?
   ANIMAL   VERB

Mr. Scaley: I feel _____ . Like I'm on top of (the)
                              ADJECTIVE

_____ .
   A PLACE

Reporter: Tell us, in your own _____ , what happened?
                                        PLURAL NOUN

Mr. Scaley: Well, it started out as a/an _____ _____
                                                  ADVERB   ADJECTIVE

morning on the lake. The fish just weren't _____ .
                                                 VERB ENDING IN "ING"

I was about to _____ up and go home when all of
                       VERB

a sudden I felt this _____ tug on my fishing _____ .
                          ADJECTIVE   NOUN

I honestly thought it was that sea monster from the legends, named

Old _____ . Turns out, it was just a really, really
        PERSON YOU KNOW

_____ _____ .
  ADJECTIVE   ANIMAL

Reporter: _____ , that's quite an amazing _____ .
                  EXCLAMATION   NOUN

Mr. Scaley: It certainly is. What a hum- _____ of a day!
                                                    SILLY WORD

From GONE FISHING MAD LIBS® • Copyright © 2024 by Penguin Random House LLC

MAD LIBS® is fun to play with friends, but you can also play it by yourself! To begin with, DO NOT look at the story on the page below. Fill in the blanks on this page with the words called for. Then, using the words you have selected, fill in the blank spaces in the story.

Now you've created your own hilarious MAD LIBS® game!

FISHERMAN'S SONG

PART OF THE BODY _____

A SOUND _____

VERB ENDING IN "ING" _____

VERB _____

PART OF THE BODY _____

PLURAL NOUN _____

ADJECTIVE _____

NOUN _____

VERB _____

ANIMAL (PLURAL) _____

PART OF THE BODY (PLURAL) _____

ADJECTIVE _____

ANIMAL (PLURAL) _____

VERB _____

OCCUPATION _____

MAD LIBS

FISHERMAN'S SONG

I bring my _____ back and let my line fly.
PART OF THE BODY

It lands with a loud _____
A SOUND

after _____ through the sky.
VERB ENDING IN "ING"

Then I wait and I _____ and I wait some more.
VERB

Who knew doing nothing could make

my _____ so sore?
PART OF THE BODY

My _____ begin to wander!
PLURAL NOUN

The _____ ways to spend
ADJECTIVE

my _____ I ponder.
NOUN

Then I _____ in my line
VERB

and notice my bait has been stolen.

Don't the _____ care
ANIMAL (PLURAL)

that my _____ are swollen?
PART OF THE BODY (PLURAL)

So I put more _____ bait on my line
ADJECTIVE

and wait again for the _____ to dine.
ANIMAL (PLURAL)

Then I wait and I _____ and I wait some more,
VERB

for I am a/an _____ down to my core.
OCCUPATION

From GONE FISHING MAD LIBS® • Copyright © 2024 by Penguin Random House LLC

MAD LIBS® is fun to play with friends, but you can also play it by yourself! To begin with, DO NOT look at the story on the page below. Fill in the blanks on this page with the words called for. Then, using the words you have selected, fill in the blank spaces in the story.

Now you've created your own hilarious MAD LIBS® game!

FISHING FAMILY

ADJECTIVE _____

NUMBER _____

COLOR _____

FIRST NAME _____

ADJECTIVE _____

OCCUPATION _____

PERSON YOU KNOW _____

SOMETHING ALIVE _____

A PLACE _____

TYPE OF BUILDING _____

ANIMAL _____

OCCUPATION _____

VEHICLE _____

ANIMAL (PLURAL) _____

COUNTRY _____

LETTER OF THE ALPHABET _____

VERB _____

OCCUPATION _____

MAD LIBS

FISHING FAMILY

I come from a/an _____ line of fisherfolk. My family has
                    ADJECTIVE

been fishing these waters for over _____ centuries. I am a direct
                                      NUMBER

descendant of the infamous _____ _____
                                 COLOR   FIRST NAME

the _____, a fisherman rumored to have also been a/an
       ADJECTIVE

_____. My great-great-uncle _____
    OCCUPATION   PERSON YOU KNOW

is a local hero. Back when he was a young _____,
                                             SOMETHING ALIVE

he managed to reel in the biggest catch (the) _____
                                                   A PLACE

had ever seen. The fish was bigger than a/an _____!
                                               TYPE OF BUILDING

His granddaughter also became a legend as the first woman to be a

female _____ _____. Even my
          ANIMAL   OCCUPATION

parents love fishing. They met on a tourist _____
                                                VEHICLE

fishing for _____ off the coast of _____.
             ANIMAL (PLURAL)   COUNTRY

Fishing is in my D- _____ -A! And that's why I love
                     LETTER OF THE ALPHABET

to _____, too. In fact, I'm such a good _____,
     VERB   OCCUPATION

I almost have gills!

From GONE FISHING MAD LIBS® • Copyright © 2024 by Penguin Random House LLC

MAD LIBS® is fun to play with friends, but you can also play it by yourself! To begin with, DO NOT look at the story on the page below. Fill in the blanks on this page with the words called for. Then, using the words you have selected, fill in the blank spaces in the story.

Now you've created your own hilarious MAD LIBS® game!

FISHING TIPS

PERSON YOU KNOW _____

PLURAL NOUN _____

OCCUPATION (PLURAL) _____

A PLACE _____

SOMETHING ALIVE (PLURAL) _____

VERB ENDING IN "ING" _____

TYPE OF FOOD _____

TYPE OF FOOD (PLURAL) _____

ADJECTIVE _____

VERB ENDING IN "S" _____

NUMBER _____

NOUN _____

ANIMAL (PLURAL) _____

NOUN _____

PLURAL NOUN _____

MAD LIBS

FISHING TIPS

My name is _____ and I'm here to share my top three
           PERSON YOU KNOW

fishing _____. Follow my advice and even you can be
      PLURAL NOUN

one of the best _____ in (the) _____.
           OCCUPATION (PLURAL)   A PLACE

_____ may be the most traditional type of
SOMETHING ALIVE (PLURAL)

_____ bait, but you can also use _____
VERB ENDING IN "ING"   TYPE OF FOOD

or _____. There's no _____ way. Do
   TYPE OF FOOD (PLURAL)   ADJECTIVE

what _____ for you. Always bring _____
     VERB ENDING IN "S"   NUMBER

rods. You never know when you might need a/an _____.
                                                                    NOUN

Remember, whether you catch a lot of _____ or not,
                                     ANIMAL (PLURAL)

at the end of the _____ you get to make up whatever
                   NOUN

story you want to! Anglers are only as good as the _____
                                                          PLURAL NOUN

they tell.

From GONE FISHING MAD LIBS® • Copyright © 2024 by Penguin Random House LLC

Join the millions of Mad Libs fans creating wacky and wonderful stories on our apps!

Download Mad Libs today!